THE HOW AND WHY WONDER BOOK OF
BALLET

Written by LEE WYNDHAM
Illustrated by RAFAELLO BUSONI
Editorial Production: DONALD D. WOLF

Edited under the supervision of
Dr. Paul E. Blackwood
U. S. Department of Health, Education and Welfare
Washington, D. C.

Text and illustrations approved by
Oakes A. White
Brooklyn Children's Museum
Brooklyn, New York

GROSSET & DUNLAP • **Publishers** • **NEW YORK**

Introduction

The world had known many forms of the dance when ballet was introduced. But this was a new kind of dance that told a story in movement and pantomime, and over the years, it has become a very highly developed and exciting art form.

The more you know about ballet, the more you can enjoy it. It helps to know how finished ballet productions depend on the cooperative efforts of many people — producers, musicians, choreographers, ballet masters, scene designers — in addition to the dancers. It helps to know that ballet is based on a few basic steps and movements with many possible variations. And it helps to know that great individual effort is required to become a successful dancer. Yet one sees that in ballet, too, success has its deep and personal satisfactions.

In ballet, the teacher is very important. New ideas and improvements have been introduced by many great ballet teachers. And as you will read here, "A great teacher is like a candle from which many other candles can be lit — so many, in fact, that the whole world can be made brighter."

The How and Why Wonder Book of Ballet is itself a teacher, and it will make the world brighter because it throws light on an exciting art form which, year by year, is becoming a more intimate and accepted part of the American scene.

Paul E. Blackwood
U. S. Department of Health, Education and Welfare
Washington, D.C.

Library of Congress Catalog Card Number: 61-12931

Contents

The Firebird, a ballet by the choreographer Michel Fokine, was first done in Paris in 1910. The composer Igor Stravinsky wrote the music for this famous ballet.

Maria Tallchief, as the magical Firebird, leaps with graceful elegance. Her power and control make her seem almost weightless in the air.

What Is Ballet?

Dancing is not only one of the oldest arts, but it is also one of our basic instincts, and a way to express our feelings. Even the smallest children dance — for joy, or with anger, or with pain — and so do grownups, for the same reasons.

But that kind of dancing is *not* ballet! The dictionary says that ballet is "a stage dance that tells a story in movement and pantomime and is performed by a group of persons."

Anyone who has seen ballet knows that this a very plain definition of the magnificent spectacle that ballet can be. Today, almost everyone has seen ballet either on television, on the movie screen, or — luckiest of all — on the

stage, performed by living, breathing dancers, so wonderfully skilled that small children have been heard to ask their mothers, "Are those people really real?"

The people are real, indeed. They move with lightness and unbelievable grace and speed because of their many years of special training in a dance form which has a technique all its own. But that is not all that makes ballet so

The Firebird and the hunter-prince who captures her do a *Pas de Deux*.

Shown are the five positions of the feet and arms on which all ballet movements are based. Every movement in ballet starts and ends in one of these basic positions. "Closed" positions: feet touch. "Open" positions: feet are parted.

wonderful to see. The other parts that make up the breath-taking whole are the finest music in the world, splendid stage scenery that stirs the imagination, glittering costumes that excite our emotions, the drama of the story, or the humor of it — for there are all kinds of ballets — or the sheer beauty of the movements of the dance.

All the creative arts are represented in ballet. It portrays not only the highest development of skill, but it is also a means of personal self-expression for many artists — those before the footlights as well as those behind the scenes.

More than that, ballet speaks to everyone who sees it in the language of movement, gesture and facial expression, which all the world can understand — without words. Therefore, ballet is a universal language which girls and boys in the United States, in France, Germany, Spain, Poland, Italy, Russia, Denmark, Sweden, Japan, Thailand, India, Africa — in fact, everywhere in the world — can enjoy. Even if all the children could be seated into some huge theater, each one, no matter what his native language, would understand the story told by the dancers.

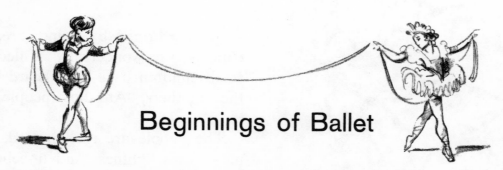

Beginnings of Ballet

Although the word "ballet" comes from the Italian *ballare,* which means "to dance," not all forms of dancing are ballet. This is because ballet is a special

kind of dancing with a technique all its own. By "technique" we refer to the things that a person needs to know and practice in order to become skillful in

an activity. It takes many years of special and difficult training to perfect ballet technique.

All the principles of ballet movement are based on the

How does ballet differ from other dancing?

plié, or knee-bend, the five formal positions of the feet, and on the "turnout" of the legs from the hip. The knee-bend enables the dancer to spring high into the air and to land like thistle-down. The all-important "turnout" allows him to move gracefully from side to side on the stage, while facing front. It also makes possible the beautiful high extensions of the legs, as in the *arabesque*. This is the foundation on which ballet is built.

But this was not the ballet of several hundred years ago.

What was early ballet like?

Then it was a form of court entertainment, really a magnificent pageant. There were no ballerinas, and all the parts were danced by men wearing masks, heavy, colorful costumes and boots or shoes. Of course, weighted down like this, the gentlemen had to dance slowly and sedately, in rows and in interesting patterns. Incidentally, they did not dance on a stage, but often mingled with their audience if no space was set aside for them in which to perform.

The first record of such an entertainment dates back to 1489, a little before Columbus discovered America. It was in honor of an Italian Duke.

Ballet was brought to France from Italy

Where did ballet come from?

about the time Catherine de Médicis married King Henry II of France. She was an expert dancer herself and adored ballet. At her wish, performers were brought from her native Italy to entertain the young queen and the court. The entertainment was a huge success. Soon, it set a new fashion, and before long the dance was imitated in every European court. But if you were to see this early dancing, you would never recognize it as the ballet you know today! In fact,

The seventeenth century court ballets were performed in a large hall, where the king and queen, seated at the head of the room, were surrounded by their household. Nobles and other members of the court sat in long galleries along the sides of the hall.

Male dancers of the eighteenth century, dressed as girls, performed at the court.

Female dancers were not permitted to perform at the time. Male dancers, dressed in the costumes of the period and wearing masks, took the assigned female roles.

some of the extravagant performances lasted as long as six hours!

Long after Catherine's time, in 1645, history records that Louis XIV danced before the royal French court. He was then seven years old! He always loved ballet and himself danced many

Where was the first ballet school started?

parts in the entertainments, including the role of the Sun King. His greatest contribution to ballet, however, was the establishment of the Royal Academy of Dancing and Music in 1661. This was the first school in the world for the instruction of ballet dancing, and even more wonderful, it has continued down to the present day at the Paris Opera.

It was in this academy that the five

were never invited to the palace spectacles, were able to see ballet.

What was the most important change in ballet? Although Louis XIV allowed women to study at the Royal Academy, they were not permitted to perform. All the dancers were still masked, and

Ballet changed when women were permitted to study at the Royal Academy, and in 1681, to perform.

positions of the classic dance were established in 1671 by the king's own dancing master, Pierre Beauchamp. It is these basic positions, refined and perfected, that are taught today!

Now ballet began to improve rapidly. **How did ballet change?** With a training school for dancers, professionals began to replace the nobles of the court, and dancing became more lively. Another change came when dancers were moved from the ballroom floor to a stage. Raised up in this way, the audience had an entirely new view of them and the movements of the dancers' feet became much more important.

Now, along with the palace performances, ballet was also performed in theaters. For the first time, people who

boys dressed as girls took the female roles. But on May 16, 1681 the most significant change of all took place. Four young ladies danced in a ballet created by the great composer, Jean-Baptiste Lully. These four were his entire class, and with them, ballerinas took their rightful place in ballet.

Early Ballerinas

The girls who studied at the Academy wore bulky clothing, tight-boned bodices, skirts that reached to the ground and heeled shoes — all of which hampered movement. But the very first ballerina was Mademoiselle Lafontaine, who made a triumphant debut in 1681. She was very beautiful and she had great charm and grace. There is very little information about her, but the great step had been taken — a ballerina was born.

Who was the first leading ballerina?

Other ballerinas followed Lafontaine, and when they retired from the stage, they taught. One of the most famous pupils was Marie

What contributions did Marie Camargo make to ballet?

Camargo, who first danced publicly in 1721. She revolutionized ballet by daring to shorten her long skirts so that her feet and lovely ankles could be seen. What's more, she had the high heels removed from her slippers. All this gave her much more freedom of movement.

She became quite famous for her jumps in the air — something ladies did not attempt before her time. So another exciting change had come to ballet. Before Camargo, the dancer scarcely moved anything more than her head and arms. She walked gracefully and she glided, but no one could see her feet. Now some of the ballet steps we know came into being, particularly the *entrechat quatre*. This is a jump into the air, with a quick changing of the legs from front to back — in her case, four times. It is a twinkling, brilliant step that is wonderful to watch.

Audiences loved Camargo. Her hair dress was copied by others, hats were named after her, as well as shoes and dresses, and even court ladies imitated her way of walking. Camargo had taken ballet off the ground.

Camargo's costume and steps altered the ballet.

Another famous ballerina was Marie Taglioni, who came from an Italian family of dancers. Her grandfather had been a dancer, her aunts and uncles were dancers. And her father, too, was a dancer, as well as a great teacher. Her mother was Swedish, however, and Marie was born in Stockholm, where her father was engaged as ballet master for the Royal Opera.

Who was Marie Taglioni?

Marie Taglioni danced in *La Sylphide,* a ballet originally created for the ballerina by her father. The ballet, first performed in 1832, is still done today.

With such a background, it is no wonder that her father decided to make a great dancer of her, even though little Marie was thin and frail. She had rather long arms and such rounded shoulders that she looked almost humpbacked. But none of this concerned Marie's father, and he packed his daughter off to study with another teacher.

Marie was a most indifferent pupil and managed to learn as little ballet as possible. A dreadful day of reckoning came, however, when she was summoned to dance before her father. As she stumbled through her exercises, he became more and more horrified. Then he set up a plan to teach her himself. This was the end of nonsense and skipping classes for Maria.

The lessons were divided into two-hour sessions, given three times daily. Poor, fragile Marie used to collapse at the end of the day. But nothing stayed the demands that her father made upon her. And then a miracle took place. At some time, during these lessons, Marie learned to like dancing!

Her debut was arranged to take place after her eighteenth birthday. Her excellent training and her unique, airy style of dancing made her an instant success. But, actually, the main subjects of the ballets of that time were not suited to her. Greek and Roman myths did not show off her airy grace, and the costumes, cluttered with drapery and trimmings, looked much too heavy. The ballet shoes were no longer heeled. They were soft slippers, but no one danced on the toes as yet.

Although Marie had captivated her Paris audience at her debut, she was to enchant them five years later. An event took place on March 12, 1832, which

made ballet different forever after — and Taglioni's dancing did it. That night, at the Paris Opera, she danced in a new ballet, *La Sylphide,* created for her especially by her father.

Before a stunned audience, the tiny dancer floated out in her white, bell-shaped dress, tight in bodice, with neck and shoulders bare. She looked truly like the nymph whose role she was performing. But what added to the illusion, besides her totally different costume, was her dancing. *She was performing on the tips of her toes* — so delicately, so lightly, she did not seem to touch the earth.

How did Marie Taglioni change ballet dancing?

Marie Taglioni had darned the tips of her limp little slippers until the arch and toe were firm. With this added support, she revolutionized ballet overnight. Her costume for that night was a long white tutu, which is still standard for what we call the "romantic" ballet. Her shoes have evolved into the toe shoes which are the dream of every little girl who takes up the study of ballet. Today, hardly anyone thinks of ballet without this dancing on the toes, yet not so long ago — less than 150 years — dancing on the toes was unheard of! Taglioni was the first to make toe dancing popular and a required accomplishment for all ballerinas.

Which ballerinas were commanded to dance for a queen?

It is often said that "comparisons are odious." It means that people do not like to be compared to others — especially if the comparison is likely to be unflattering! Well, in her time, Taglioni was not the only famous dancer. There were others whom audiences adored just as much. There were Carlotta Grisi, Fannie Cerito and Lucile Grahn — all of whom had earned considerable acclaim in England in individual performances. Queen Victoria decided that she would like to see the world's four greatest ballerinas perform together! An invitation to perform before royalty is called "a command performance," and it is practically unheard of for anyone or any group to refuse such a command.

But handling four delicately tempered ballerinas must have been a great ordeal for everyone concerned. The famous ladies danced just one performance of the specially created *Pas de Quatre* — Dance for Four — before the Queen, and then refused ever to appear together again!

Ballerinas now were stars, with devoted audiences and important dignitaries vying with each other to bring them tokens of appreciation. Ballerinas were cheered wildly and sometimes borne through the streets on the shoulders of their admirers. Carriage horses were unhitched and the carriages drawn by enthusiastic young men.

One story tells of Taglioni's visit to Russia. After her performance there, some Russians bought her toe shoes for a huge price. They then stewed them in a pot and solemnly drank the broth in her honor!

But what had become of the once all-important male dancers? At this time they seemed to have faded into the scenery. All the public attention was focused on the ballerinas. The magnificent strength of the men, their ability to leap high and wide and to support the ballerina while she showed off her varied skills, was seldom used.

Did male dancers perform during this period?

Ballet in Russia

The Russians were so impressed by Taglioni's dancing that the French ballet teachers at the Russian schools began to train their own pupils to dance her roles and to duplicate her style.

Then a group of Italian dancers came to Russia and astounded the audiences there by their tremendous jumps and turns and general air of liveliness and vitality. Virginia

What contributions to ballet were made by Italian dancers?

At the Command Performance for Queen Victoria of England in 1845, four leading ballerinas of the day performed in a *Pas de Quatre*, especially created for them. The dancers were Taglioni, Carlotta Grisi, Fannie Cerito and Lucile Grahn.

Zucchi's audiences were breathless when she performed her steps. The Russians promptly invited Enrico Cecchetti to teach them the brilliant Italian style of dancing.

After Zucchi came Pierina Legani. She set the dance world agog with her performance of continuous multiple turns called *fouettés*. She made a series of thirty-two of these sensational whipping turns around the stage. The people applauded so enthusiastically that she at once repeated the feat. The cheers of that audience have echoed down to the present time.

For many years thereafter, thirty-two *fouettés* remained the wonder of the ballet world. They were performed by only a few accomplished dancers. Today, however, this is no longer considered extraordinary, though it remains a part of the dance vocabulary of every advanced student. Thirty-two, or even sixty-four *fouettés* are still exciting to see, even if they are no longer a great wonder. You may have seen a ballerina on television or in a theater who spins about like a top and then stops short, not even out of breath, to take her bow. Well, it takes more than this whipping about the stage without getting dizzy to make a ballerina — but it is showy!

The importance of Zucchi and Legani is their effect on Russian ballet. Now the Russian teachers and composers, many of whom were French or Italian by birth, combined the old French movements of slow grace and beauty with the vibrant Italian technique. As time went on, this was blended with the native qualities of Russian ballet. Now this is called the Russian style of ballet.

For many years it was held up as the symbol of ballet perfection to the rest of the world.

This kind of dancing became known as the "classic" ballet. To show it off to its best advantage, a special costume known as the classic *tutu* was designed. It was cut so very short that the dancers' legs were free to execute the new vigorous turns and leaps devised for the classic ballets.

What costume was designed for the classic ballet?

Russian Ballet Dancers

The fame of the Italian ballet had begun to fade when ballet in Russia took on new life. Russian-born ballerinas suddenly leaped to stardom in the ballet world.

14

An exquisite *prima ballerina* of the Russian Imperial Ballet was Olga Preobrajenska. But she was surpassed by Mathilde Kchessinskaya — tiny, light as air itself, and perfect. In fact, by order of the Imperial Court, she was granted the title of *prima ballerina assoluta,* which was another way of saying, "the first and most absolutely perfect ballerina."

Which ballerina got a special title from the Czar of Russia?

Of course, some ballerinas who came after her would have earned the same grand title. But by that time Russia was in the midst of a terrible revolution and the Czar had been killed. As the Imperial Court no longer existed, no such title could be granted by it again. Thus, Kchessinskaya was the only dancer to get this title from the Czar.

She became the wife of a Grand Duke, which gave her added influence in the ballet world. However, when the Revolution broke out, she had to flee Russia. She settled in Paris and opened a ballet school there.

Many of the ballets perfected in her day are still presented, and will most probably be enjoyed in future generations as well. *Giselle, The Sleeping Beauty, Coppélia,* and *The Nutcracker* have qualities to keep them popular.

The Russian ballerina who became the most famous in the world was Anna Pavlova. She is still a household word, and girls the world over dream of "dancing like Pavlova." Anna was only seven when her mother took her to a ballet performance as a Christmas treat. Then and there the child fell in love with the dance. But she was not old enough even to try to enter the famous Imperial School. She had to wait two long years to do so.

How did Pavlova become a dancer?

In the Imperial School the children received their training and school lessons free, because the school was supported by the Czar. However, applicants were chosen with the greatest care and had to pass a stiff examination to be admitted. This included appearance, good health, natural grace, a feeling for music and rhythm, and intelligence. The fortunate ones were given a year to prove themselves. They had to show real progress to be allowed to stay.

How the frail little Anna ever passed the health test is a mystery, but pass she did. And progress she did. Her

Anna Pavlova (foreground) and other pupils took ballet lessons at the famous Imperial School in Russia.

15

Anna Pavlova performed her unforgettable role in the ballet *The Dying Swan*. It was choreographed by Michel Fokine to the music of French composer Camille Saint-Saëns, and was the ballerina's most famous creation.

Vaslav Nijinsky was noted for his sensational leaps, which were unequaled then as now. At the top of the page are shown Nijinsky and Anna Pavlova in one of their memorable performances with the noted Ballet Russe company in France.

fragile, sensitive beauty cast a spell of enchantment wherever she danced. People still speak of her with reverence.

Many present-day ballerinas are said to be more perfect than Pavlova. In her own day she never performed the showy thirty-two *fouettés,* or multiple *pirouettes.* Yet she became the unofficial *prima ballerina assoluta* of the world. It never mattered to her public what she danced. It was *how* she danced that made her the symbol of ballet to millions of people throughout the world.

She had a personal magic that transported her audience. She was light, airy, and danced effortlessly and radiantly. She could be a sylph, or a cloud or she could be touched with fire almost real enough to set everything around her ablaze.

Even reading about the way she performed *The Dying Swan* has brought

What was Pavlova's most famous dance?

tears to many an eye. She floated across the stage in tiny *bourrés* (fluttering, weaving steps), she curved her lovely neck, her body trembled, she sank . . . and died . . . and people wept.

Anna Pavlova brought ballet to the whole world. She traveled everywhere, meeting schedules that would make strong men turn pale. This fragile ballerina was made of something much stronger than steel. She took by storm England, France, the United States. She went to Egypt, South Africa, Burma, Costa Rica, Malay, Australia, Java. Hundreds of thousands of miles, thousands of performances, millions saw her dance. Her name seems engraved in the public minds, and today ballet might just as well be spelled "pavlova."

Vaslav Nijinsky also studied in the Imperial School, and he was one of Pavlova's several partners. His dancing was superb, strong and manly. On stage he seemed illuminated by some inner fire. The most difficult steps were easy for him. His leaps were sensational. When he was asked how he performed them, he said that it was quite simple. "You merely pause a little in the air — and then come down again." He was the most famous male dancer of all time.

Who was the most famous male dancer of all time?

Of course Nijinsky was only joking when he said he paused in the air. It just happened that he possessed extraordinary physical strength and had splendid training. At the peak of his leaps, he thrust his legs out further — and it was this which made him appear to pause in the air. He had something else, too, a God-given talent, that special ingredient which makes people great in their own special fields whether they be dancers, teachers, musicians, writers or baseball players.

How did Nijinsky manage his leaps?

Serge Diaghilev was not a dancer. He was a cultured gentleman who loved ballet. At the turn of the twentieth century he felt that ballet was no longer making any prog-

Who was Serge Diaghilev?

ress. The same things were being done over and over again — long ballets in lavish settings and complicated stories of unearthly beings.

Ballet had become bogged down by tradition. Tradition is a fine thing to build on, but certainly it is not good to live completely in the past and ignore the needs and developments of the present.

True, we still know and love some of these ballets and thrill to the beautiful music of Tschaikovsky, as in *The Sleeping Beauty*. But this ballet has been revamped for the modern taste. The same is true of *Swan Lake,* where most usually only the second act is given.

Diaghilev did not like the rivalries that existed among the ballerinas. Instead of concentrating on fine expression in their dancing and characteriza-

tion, they vied with one another in feats of technical brilliance. Night after night in the famous Maryinsky Theater he could hear people softly counting the number of *pirouettes* (a turn or sequence of turns on one foot) or *fouettés* made by their favorite dancers.

Although today we realize that ballet is a combination of several arts — technical ballet skill, music and art — in Diaghilev's day no one thought of creating ballet as a combined whole!

Ballet creators searched for suitable

How were ballets created during Diaghilev's time?

stories. Then they arranged steps that would tell these stories. When the dancers started to learn the steps, costume and scenery designers went to work. They were told what the ballet was about, but they never discussed any of their plans with the choreographers, who are the creators of the ballet steps. What is more, when the leading dancers learned their parts, they often asked to have steps and movements left out, because these did not happen to show them off to their best advantage. To fill in the gap, sometimes they were allowed to put in steps they liked from some other ballet.

Nijinsky was the slave Zobeïdas in the ballet *Scheherazade,* with music by Rimsky-Korsakov, done in 1910.

Diaghilev did not approve of this at all. He felt that all the artists who made up a ballet company should work together and unify all their efforts into one glorious whole. He was not alone in this opinion.

A young dancer and choreographer, Michel Fokine, who had created *The Dying Swan* dance for Pavlova in 1905, felt exactly as Diaghilev did. But when he proposed new ideas to his superiors at the Imperial Theater, they were rejected. Thus, when Diaghilev decided to form a company of Russian dancers to take to Paris, Fokine was very glad to go along as its choreographer.

The Ballet Russe

Diaghilev was a great and imaginative impresario. An "impresario" is the organizer or manager of a concert company, but Diaghilev was much more than that. He was a genius who could inspire groups of highly temperamental artists to work together toward a common goal. He was not so much concerned with box office profits as he was with perfection. And his company was artistically perfect. It was on May 18, 1909 that Diaghilev's Ballet Russe opened for its first season in Paris.

Diaghilev's principal dancers were

Who were the main artists of Diaghilev's Ballet Russe?

Anna Pavlova, Tamara Karsavina and Vaslav Nijinsky. Young Michel Fokine was his choreographer. His designers, costumers and musicians were the finest in Russia. Everyone in his company contributed his or her talent to a final brilliant result. No wonder their ballet season was such a tremendous success. Not only the first season, but the next and the next and the next — for twenty wonderful years! It was one great spectacle after another.

Of course, the company changed from time to time. Dancers accepted concert engagements or left to form companies and schools of their own. But wherever they went, they carried with them the Diaghilev influence.

Among the male dancers in Diaghilev's company were Mordkin, Volinine, Massine, Dolin, Lifar. Fokine performed as well as created, and Cecchetti took on numerous character roles, including Charlatan in the ballet *Petrouchka*.

The clown Petrouchka was one of the four principals of the production.

Diaghilev constantly sought out and encouraged talented people. Among his composers — and ballet has some of the finest music in the world — were Debussy, Ravel, Richard Strauss, Stravinsky, Fauré, Prokofiev and many others.

His designers included such famous painters as Picasso, Benois, Bakst, Matisse and others.

And among his choreographers were Fokine, Nijinsky, Massine, Nijinska and George Balanchine, who became the artistic director of the world-famous New York City Ballet.

It was Fokine who changed the nature of the stories that ballet told. He changed the style of dancing, too, by introducing vivid, living characters to the dance. What is more, he helped

What contributions did Michel Fokine make to the ballet?

initiate the idea of using music as part of the ballet itself, rather than a mere accompaniment to the dancing.

A good example of this new way to use music is in the ballet *Petrouchka*, which is a story of puppets come to life. The music is part of the action itself. The instruments seem to quarrel when the characters do. The orchestra "shrieks" when the puppet Petrouchka is supposed to shriek. This music is by Stravinsky, and the dances were created by Fokine.

Dancers never stop learning and trying to perfect their art. Diaghilev engaged the great Imperial School teacher Enrico Cecchetti to instruct his dancers. Although Cecchetti was delightfully sociable in everyday life, in the classroom he was a strict disciplinarian. He

Who taught the dancers of the Ballet Russe?

Egorova, Nijinska (the sister of Vaslav Nijinsky), and Alicia Markova, to mention just a few. (Diaghilev engaged this English girl for his company when she was only fourteen years old.)

One of the most popular productions of

What other ballets were presented by the Ballet Russe?

the Ballet Russe was, and still is, *Firebird*. This is a very colorful ballet of a glorious bird with magic powers, of a wicked magician, a princess held captive and a handsome prince who finally rescues and marries her.

The ballet *Le Spectre de la Rose* is not so much story as beautiful dancing.

In Fokine's *Petrouchka,* with music by Stravinsky, the Sorcerer (left) brings to life the puppets Petrouchka, the Ballerina, and the Moor (below).

was never satisfied with mere technical perfection. He demanded complete understanding of their roles from the dancers, coupled with an inner glow, a fire, which made their dancing memorable. Under his guidance, the dancing reached the perfection Diaghilev demanded, and all the ballets were performed exactly as they were planned by the choreographers!

No matter how harsh Cecchetti might have been with the dancers in his classes, all his pupils remembered him kindly. He helped develop the talents of many ballet stars still active today — and through them the talents of younger dancers they, in turn, have taught. A great teacher is like a candle from which many other candles can be lit — so many, in fact, that the whole world can be made brighter.

Besides those already mentioned, Cecchetti taught Danilova, Sokolova,

A young girl has returned from a ball. When she takes off her cape, we see that she is still holding a red rose that was given to her by her sweetheart. Holding it close, she dances dreamily. Then she sinks into a chair and falls asleep. At this moment, the rose comes to life and executes a magnificent dance. Then, as dawn lights up the window, the rose says farewell to the girl and, in what seems like a never-ending leap, soars out through the casements. This was one of Nijinsky's famous leaps, and he was the first to dance this role to Fokine's choreography. The ballerina was Tamara Karsavina.

The ballet *Prince Igor* served to introduce Western Europe to the color, music and dancing of Russia. The music is from the second act of an opera by Alexander Borodin. This ballet has no connection with the plot of the opera. It is just wonderful music, setting and dancing, showing dance artists in native costume performing with unbelievable energy, speed and vigor.

Diaghilev toured Europe and America, and everywhere that his troupe danced, there was both an upsurge of interest in ballet and a tremendous acclaim for his company. By the time Serge Diaghilev died in 1929, the whole world had been influenced by his idea of what ballet should be. The seeds for present-day dancing, which he had helped to ripen, were now scattered everywhere in the form of his dancers, musicians and choreographers — and from them grew ballet as we know it today.

Ballet Today

Because people before us had freed ballet of meaningless conventions and had not been afraid to experiment with new ideas, we now can enjoy all kinds of ballet — romantic, classic and modern. There are ballets which tell dramatic or tragic stories as well as ballets which are filled with humor. There are also ballets which express only a mood in music and motion and ballets that are rich in color and brilliance. Often you can see examples of each on the same theater program, as for example, *Swan Lake, Firebird, Afternoon of a Faun,* and *Western Symphony.*

All ballet training is classical. That is,

What is classic ballet? it is based on a standard of rules which evolved from the Academy of Dance established by Louis XIV. The student learns a basic "vocabulary" of steps from which countless variations can be made so that all kinds of movement are possible.

The classic dance is fundamental material out of which new ballets can be made, and it gives the dancer a sure knowledge to draw on when he is required to perform a work that is new to him.

When you see a ballet listed on the program as "classic," it does not mean, therefore, that this is going to be something old. What it really means is that here is an example of the finest of its kind. That is precisely what classic means: "a work of the highest class and acknowledged excellence."

Therefore, ballets can be romantic and classic as well as modern and classic, because they combine the knowledge and skills developed over the centuries which have been handed down, teacher to pupil, to our own time.

Probably the most popular among the

What are some classic ballets?

classic ballets is *Swan Lake*. It is performed by almost every company in the world. The story is about a beautiful girl, Odette, who is transformed by a magician into a swan

queen. Only at midnight, for one brief hour, can she resume her human form. It is then that a prince and his friends, out on a hunt, discover her. As Odette begs the prince not to shoot her swans, he falls in love with her. Some of the most beautiful dancing can be seen in this ballet, and it is the ambition of every ballerina to dance the role of Odette.

A motion picture, in color, was made of this ballet by The Royal Ballet Company of England, and it affords a magnificent view of classic dancing. Odette is danced here by Margot Fonteyn, prima ballerina of the company. The prince is Michael Somes, also one of England's greatest dancers.

The Sleeping Beauty is a classic bal-

The bar helps dancers keep their balance when they learn and practice.

Pupils of a present-day ballet school exercise at the bar — or *barre*.

23

let which is based on the well-known fairy tale of the same name. Moira Shearer of England makes a beautiful Princess Aurora. Perhaps you have seen her dance in the motion picture entitled *The Red Shoes*.

The Nutcracker is often performed at Christmas time, but if you can't see it on a living stage, remember that it is often given on television during the holiday season. The ballet opens with a family Christmas party, and there is a large, richly decorated Christmas tree in the setting. The best present, as far as little Clara is concerned, is a cleverly devised Nutcracker which looks like a soldier — the gift of her rather mysterious godfather.

That night, when the party is over, Clara dreams that the Nutcracker has come to life as a charming young prince.

He takes her to Fairyland, through the Snow Country and into the Kingdom of the Sugarplum Fairy. There a grand celebration is held in Clara's honor. The subjects of the Queen perform many dances to Tschaikovsky's beautiful flowing music. There are Spanish Dancers, Candy Canes, an Arabian Dancer, Mother Ginger and her delightful little children, Flowers and Sugar Angels. Finally the Sugarplum Fairy and her Prince dance a *grand pas de deux* — a dance for two — and that is when children whisper to their mothers, "Are those people really real?"

With Nicholas Magallanes for a partner, Maria Tallchief as the Sugarplum Fairy exhibits some of the finest classic dancing for which George Balanchine's New York City Ballet Company is famous.

The Prince falls in love with the Swan Queen in Marius Petipa's *Swan Lake*. The music is by Tschaikovsky.

Clara is taken to the Kingdom of the Sugarplum Fairy in *The Nutcracker*.

Clara dreams that the Nutcracker, a gift from her godfather, comes alive.

What are romantic ballets? The ballets we call "romantic" are a kind of classical ballet. They are romantic in mood. The desire to express this mood and to give the dancers more of the appearance of spirit-like creatures was responsible for the development of toe dancing. It is in these romantic ballets that dancers first rose to the tips of their toes.

It was at this time, also, that the white ballet, or *ballet blanc*, came into being — and the delicate, romantic *tutu* we know in such productions as *Giselle, Swan Lake* and *Les Sylphides* was created.

Which is the most popular of the romantic ballets? *Giselle* is the story of a peasant girl who falls in love with Duke Albrecht, who has disguised himself as a peasant. When the girl discovers his real identity and learns that he is engaged to marry a princess, she loses her mind and dies of grief.

In the second act, the remorseful prince visits her grave at night. The cemetery is haunted by the wilis, spirits of brides-to-be who have died before

Alicia Markova as Giselle and Anton Dolin as Duke Albrecht dance in the ballet *Giselle*. The romantic ballet was originally performed in the year 1841 in Paris and is the work of the composer A. C. Adam.

their wedding day. Now they appear, with Giselle among them, and force her to dance with Albrecht. Dawn comes in time to save him from ill fate.

This ballet, the most popular of the romantic ones, was first produced in Paris in 1841. It is the "Hamlet" of the ballet world. Just as every actor wants to play Hamlet, so every ballerina wants to dance the part of Giselle and bring to the role her own particular gifts and interpretation.

In our time, Giselle was danced by Alicia Markova, Margot Fonteyn, Alicia Alonso, Moira Shearer, Ulanova, the Russian prima ballerina and many others.

Some of the modern ballets of today **What is modern ballet?** tell a story. When they do, the costumes and scenery fit the period and setting of that story. Other modern ballets express only a mood or a feeling. In that case, the costumes and settings are designed for line and color and to fit the mood or feeling to be expressed.

The movements of many of these ballets, at first glance, might look nothing at all like those of the classic and romantic ballets. In some of these ballets the dancers use straight movements of the arms rather than the rounded classic ones. Body lines are sometimes angular.

Yet the modern ballet dancer begins training in exactly **How are modern ballet dancers trained to dance?** the same way as the earlier dancers did — with the five positions of the feet, the ninety-degree turnout of the leg from the hip, and all the other exercises which give the body suppleness, grace and balletic ease of movement. Then the acquiring of modern steps to fit the specific new dances is easy. The vocabulary — or visible language of ballet — has been used in each era to express that particular time. Once it was full of pomp and circumstance. Then it was filled with the romantic qualities of the nineteenth century, followed by the realist presenta-

26

tions of Fokine and Diaghilev. Now it is crisp with modern designs and the dreams and realities of today's world.

What are some modern ballets? Probably the best known modern American ballet is Agnes De Mille's *Rodeo*. Set in the Southwest, on a ranch, it deals with a tomboy's desperate efforts to attract the attention of the Head Cowboy. All her attempts to charm him with her cowgirl skills fall into ridicule until she sees the error of her ways. Everything changes when she appears dressed as a girl, with becoming feminine manners. Now the Head Cowboy dances right up to her, but she chooses the Champion Roper instead. Of all the people on the ranch, he, alone, was kind to her earlier when she behaved so foolishly.

Rodeo was first presented in New York on October 16, 1942 — and at that moment a great American choreographer was discovered. Nothing like it had ever been seen before, and from that moment, the particular style of dancing presented by Agnes De Mille became part of the American dance scene. She, herself, danced the part of the Cowgirl. Frederic Franklin was the Champion Roper.

Other ballets designed by Agnes De Mille were included in the motion pictures *Oklahoma* and *Carousel*. These were musical plays first and toured the country, playing before enthusiastic audiences everywhere. The ballets were woven right into the story and many people who had never seen ballet before, decided that they liked it. It wasn't highbrow and stuffy at all!

Some of the steps done in ballet are shown below. Their names are in French, for it was in France that ballet grew.

PIROUETTE PASSÉ

PIROUETTE

ARABESQUE

ARABESQUE

RELEVÉ

RELEVÉ PASSÉ

DÉVELOPPÉ À LA SECONDE

GRAND JETÉ

The Cowgirl, looking like a tomboy, kicks out with displeasure when she is ignored.

The Head Cowboy and the Rancher's Daughter.

A modern ballet that is quite different is *Graduation Ball*. This is set in a fashionable girls' school in Vienna. A gala entertainment is arranged for the graduates of a nearby military academy. When the girls and boys meet, there are some awkward moments. The boys are bashful, the girls are shy. Somebody falls down and is horribly embarrassed. But then the party gets under way and everyone has fun, including the headmistress and the pompous old general.

The ballet *Fancy Free* is about three American sailors on shore leave in New York. It was created by choreographer Jerome Robbins, with composer Leonard Bernstein. The slapstick humor and clever dance steps always have audiences laughing at the sailors' antics.

Not to be outdone, the British navy has to be remembered in modern ballet, too. It is done in *Pineapple Poll,* which is based on Gilbert and Sullivan operettas. The story of this ballet is taken from Gilbert's ballad, *The Bumboat Woman's Story*. A bumboat, by the way, is a boat that carries provisions — fruit, vegetables, trinkets — out to ships at anchor. Pineapple Poll is a pretty young girl who stows away aboard the *HMS Hot Cross Bun,* in order to be near Captain Belaye. Then she discovers that also aboard are a number of other very un-sailor-like sailors, who turn out to be girls with the identical idea she has! It is quite a situation, especially when the Captain brings aboard his new bride. The "sailors" fall over in a mass faint — but eventually all ends well.

Elaine Fifield was the first to dance

Pineapple Poll. David Blair was Captain Belaye.

Serge Prokofiev, who wrote *Peter and the Wolf* as a musical fairy tale to teach children the difference between various instruments in the orchestra, also wrote the music for *Gala Performance*. This is a spoof on ballet, a comedy, involving three self-important ballerinas from three different countries who consent to dance together.

Just before the actual performance, the three stars appear on stage one by one. First comes the Russian, the Queen of the Dance, a haughty overdressed lady. Then the sparkling French ballerina runs on, wearing a fluffy costume. She at once tells the conductor what kind of tempo she expects from him. She seems to talk, talk, talk. Now comes the Italian ballerina, famed as Goddess of the Dance. She is overpoweringly dignified, and walks as if not sure the floor beneath is worthy to receive her precious footsteps. All this time the boys and girls of the *corps de ballet* are watching from the background, convulsed with laughter.

The performance of the trio is in keeping with their established characters — exaggerated and ridiculous. And at the end, the ladies practically fight over the applause.

When first given in the United States, the cast was headed by Nora Kay, Nana Gollner, Karen Conrad, Hugh Laing, and Antony Tudor, who also did the choreography for this ballet.

The popular, modern ballets *Fancy Free, Graduation Ball* and *Pineapple Poll* were originally performed in New York, Sydney, Australia and London, respectively.

FANCY FREE

GRADUATION BALL

PINEAPPLE POLL

In this scene from Serge Prokofiev's ballet *Peter and the Wolf*, the Wolf is shown chasing the Bird.

The Russian, French and Italian ballerinas have their "say" in the ballet *Gala Performance*. The music is by the composer Serge Prokofiev.

What is character dancing? In ballet, roles which require dramatic interpretation are called character parts. Sometimes these roles require character dancing, completely in keeping with the person or creature being portrayed. Sometimes, no dancing is required, and the character merely walks about the stage performing his role. In *Coppélia*, the owner of the life-size doll is Dr. Coppelius. This character role has been played by the gifted Robert Helpmann. Perhaps you have seen him in the motion picture *Tales of Hoffman* in which he played the character role of the wicked Dr. Miracle.

The Mother in *Giselle* is a character role. In *The Nutcracker*, Clara's godfather, Drosselmeyer, is a character — white-haired, sinister, with a black patch over one eye! In the magnificent *Firebird*, the wicked magician, Kastchei, was played by the famous Enrico Cecchetti of the Diaghilev company.

In *The Sleeping Beauty*, Frederick Ashton portrays the wicked fairy Carabosse. It is a ballet tradition that the roles of ugly, grotesque or evil old women should usually be played by men.

Character dancing also includes national folk dances adapted for ballet, such as the polka or the Italian *Tarantella*. Scottish, Spanish, Russian, Irish — any kind of national dance may be adapted to give the flavor of those countries to parts of various ballets.

Pantomime—a Language of the Dance

What is pantomime? To help the audience understand the emotions in a dance, many pantomime gestures have been developed. That is, gestures of the hands, facial expressions and the general attitude of the body. Done with restraint, they can express serious feeling, but a clever character dancer can transform them into anything he wants with a slight exaggeration. When you become familiar with the pantomime samples given here, watch for them in the ballet performances you see and notice how they are used. This awareness will add greatly to your enjoyment.

For example, to express *love*, the dancer holds both hands over the heart.

A *wish to marry* is expressed by pointing to the wedding-ring finger with the index finger of the right hand.

To say *I*, the dancer points toward himself with the middle fingers of both hands.

For *you*, he points to the person with an open hand. If angry, then he points with the finger in a violent gesture.

Beautiful or *girl* is expressed by circling the face gently with the back of the hand. The back of the middle finger outlines the face.

An invitation to *dance* is expressed by circling the hands around each other above the head.

For a *kiss*, the lips are touched with the finger.

Stop is such a universal gesture, it is the same the world over—and in dance, too. Here the performer holds up the hand, palm out.

Anger is expressed by raising the arms above the head, with the elbows to the front, and shaking fists.

A command to *obey* is shown by pointing to the floor with a very decided gesture.

To say *no*, the dancer holds the arms at the side, then crosses them before the body in a definite gesture as he shakes his head.

A dancer who wants to say that he *forgot*, will hold the hands out loosely, palms up, and shake the head slightly.

When he *remembers*, he holds the index finger to the temple.

To say *friends*, the dancer clasps the hands together on a level with the waist.

For *sadness*, the dancer traces tears running down the face with his fingers.

For actual *weeping*, he hides the face in both hands, or rubs his eyes with clenched fists.

DR. COPPELIUS IN *COPPÉLIA*

MADGE, THE WITCH, IN *LA SYLPHIDE*

ASTROLOGER IN *COQ D'OR*

SPANISH FOLK DANCER

To *beg for mercy*, the dancer holds the arms out, palms together as if praying.

A *blessing* is given with the hands touching the head of the person blessed.

Sleep is indicated by inclining the head against the back of the hands.

A *child* is indicated with the palms of the hands. The dancer raises the palms in three steps, as if measuring the height of a growing child.

Thank you is shown very simply by inclining the head. One hand is brought down from a position on the chest and extended toward the person thanked.

A *king* is indicated by a flourishing gesture and the raising of the right hand above the head to indicate a feather plume, which is usually worn in the hats of nobility.

A *queen* is shown by the index finger of the right hand touching the top of the forehead at points where a crown would touch the head.

This type of pantomime is used for the most part in the older, classical ballets and if you know it, you will understand the stories more clearly. Watch for it especially on television and in movies, where the dancers are brought so close to the viewer, you can even see the flicker of an eyelash.

People Who Make Ballet

The ballet productions you see from "out front" — in the audience — didn't just happen. They were created and made possible by people, many of whom are never seen by the public and many whose names never appear on the program.

Producing a ballet, and paying all the expenses and salaries involved requires a vast outlay of money. In the past, kings and queens supported royal ballet companies. Today, many ballet companies overseas are supported by the government. Though governments in those countries may have changed from time to time, each successive one has continued to support not only the ballet companies, but ballet schools also. Talented young people are able to get a classic ballet education and an academic education on a scholarship basis.

Who supports the ballet companies?

France, through all her political troubles, has continued to maintain the academy founded by Louis XIV. The Russian Academy, founded by the Czars, continues under Communism. Italy, Denmark, Sweden and Austria give ballet official support. And recently Great Britain has begun to subsidize a national ballet.

Some South American countries, which have taken great strides forward in many cultural directions, now support ballet. And in Mexico, the government not only supports the arts, but pays dance students while they go to school.

Who supports ballet in the United States?

In the United States, dance students study at their own expense, although many privately-owned schools offer scholarships to promising students. The cost of many years of study is high, and dancing schools are completely separate from institutions of academic studies. However, in New York City there are two public high schools which are devoted to the arts. One is the High School of Performing Arts, the other is the High School of Music and Art. Here the arts can be studied and perfected while one is still very young.

Many people hope that some day the United States will have a National Foundation for the performing arts, which will give qualified young people from even the smallest towns and hamlets a chance to perfect their talents.

In the United States, ballet depends on private individuals to underwrite the huge expenses of productions. It also depends on "patrons" — people who contribute various sums annually toward the support of their favorite company. Actually, you also help to support a company each time you buy a ticket.

An "angel" in theater language, is a person who puts up all or part of the money to make a production possible. The greater his investment in a production which becomes a financial success, the greater his profit.

33

Every company needs an executive director — a company manager — to supervise everything. He usually has assistants, for no one person could even hope to take care of all the details alone. Also, with so many temperamental artists involved, it is advisable to have a company "Solomon" who is tactful enough to settle noisy disputes. The manager has that job, too.

What is the job of the company manager?

The artistic director takes charge of the ballet as a work of art. He brings out the best in his artists, overcomes the worst and develops all the potentials. He does not spare himself — or anyone else — and makes everyone work harder than they thought possible. He "lives" each part and helps each dancer interpret his or her role properly. They must perform up to his ideals and standards, and it is this factor which gives a particular company its distinctive character.

What job does the artistic director do?

The choreographer creates the dances. He is an artist who works with motion. He searches for the basic movements which express the emotion behind the

What is the role of the choreographer?

human experience of his story. Then he translates these movements into the meaningful language of ballet. A choreographer must be a dancer — and a good one. This has always been true. All the distinguished choreographers of the past were fine dancers in their own right. They studied ballet technique for many years, joined ballet companies and danced many roles. They associated with designers, musicians, other dancers — learning all the while, observing, absorbing all kinds of knowledge. They also studied history, art and music as well as the world of human emotion around them. Whenever possible, they traveled and studied the dances of other lands. The choreogra-

pher of today does precisely the same thing to prepare himself for his profession.

There are no schools in which choreography can be taught. Schools can teach technique, they can outline a course of study, but the would-be choreographer has to develop his own special talents.

The choreographer must have infinite patience and the ability to teach others, because he has to show his dancers how to perform certain movements which he has created. He must have a clear understanding of the steps and movements a dancer can and cannot do. That is why he must be a dancer himself.

In the course of gathering his own

experience, the choreographer becomes a walking encyclopedia of dances, dance steps and many ideas for using them. He is usually a tireless perfectionist, as minor faults cause him agonies, even though no one else is aware of them. But that is how one arrives at perfection — by taking infinite pains over the smallest details.

The choreographer is a creative artist, and he is expected constantly to produce something new, something surprising, something beautiful. Very often he does!

What is a ballet master? Although the choreographer and the artistic director can demonstrate the steps and movements they want from their dancers, it is the ballet master — or ballet mistress — who sees to it that they learn them exactly. Many, many hours are spent in such rehearsals, first in rehearsal halls, then in the theater itself.

How does a composer serve in the ballet? A composer creates or arranges music for the ballet. How this is worked out depends on how the choreographer gets his idea for the ballet. If the story or mood comes first, then suitable music must either be written or arranged from existing scores. If a ballet is to be written to existing music, then this is arranged to fit the steps devised by the choreog-

rapher. Either way, there must be close association and understanding between these two persons.

There must be an orchestra to play the music of the composer. So there must be musicians and a conductor to see to it that the music is learned and played in the tempo indicated by the choreographer.

What is the job of a wardrobe mistress in a ballet company? It is said that the wardrobe mistress was born with a needle and thread in her hand, but her feeling for and knowledge of ballet and ballet people sometimes suggests that there is dancer's blood in her veins. In a ballet company she is indispensable. Her rule is over all the costumes — for lords and ladies, witches, knights, goblins and fairies, snowflakes and sunbeams, waltzing flowers, nutcrackers and toys which come to life. She keeps buttons on, moths out, starch in. She folds and packs with secret tricks against crushing. She labels and puts away — and finds what she wants when she wants it. She is ingenious when it comes to cleaning, patching or mending. At performance time she hooks, zips, ties, nips a waist in, takes a tuck out, fluffs,

The scene designer builds a miniature stage for the ballet after he has drawn sketches of the scenery.

smooths down. She scolds, she comforts, she prays, too. One thing is certain—without her there would be chaos in the dressing rooms.

The scenery is designed and planned

What part does a scene designer play in ballet?

by an artist, first on paper, then on a miniature stage. It is very important to have the background suit the story of the ballet. At the same time, it is very important to have the scenery so designed that dancers can come on and off the stage and perform without catching their costumes awkwardly. Nor must they be crowded or overshadowed by the sets.

Lighting effects are also very important and are planned most carefully. Incorrect lighting can completely spoil the mood of a ballet, wash color out of

costumes or change them from beauty into ugliness. On the other hand, a simple backdrop curtain can be made to look like "scenery" by clever lighting.

Costumes must be designed to harmo-

In what way does a costume designer aid ballet dancers?

nize with the scenery and to fit the story. But there are many more considerations than this. To begin with, the designer must remember that a dancer has to move in a costume — and no matter how forcefully, costume and dancer must not part company.

Also, the costume must not be draped in such a way that it becomes a trap — catching a foot in a leap, flying across the face and obscuring vision or taking pieces of scenery with it.

To guard against these nightmares that haunt both dancers and designers, many conferences and fittings take place with the designer, dancers, dressmaker, choreographer and the set designer.

The stage manager is completely responsible for the operation of each performance. He has to know a great many things in order to cue the light crew and the curtain men. From the moment he orders, "Places, everybody!" to the echo of the last applause, he is like a captain at the helm, keeping everything under control and maintaining the pace of the show. His wits must be sharp and ever ready to cope with any emergency that might arise.

What does the stage manager do?

The property man is in charge of the scenery and the props. He oversees the stage manager, takes care of the proper lighting effects for each scene and oversees the men working the spotlights. The carpenter is in charge of all the carpentry to be done on the sets. The flyman oversees the raising and lowering of the huge backdrops for the settings. The curtainman raises and lowers the curtain at the right moments, on cue from the stage manager.

Who are some other important backstage help?

Dancers wait for their cue in the wings of the stage or behind the scenery while a performance is in progress.

Present-day Ballerinas and Danseurs

The radiant Queen of the Royal Ballet,
Margot Fonteyn Margot Fonteyn, is
as popular in the
United States as she is in England. Her
ballet technique is so perfect that her
dancing appears effortless and spon-
taneous.

Her father, a mining engineer, was
a Yorkshire man and her mother of
Brazilian-Irish extraction, which probably accounts for Fonteyn's exotic
beauty. As a child she traveled over
much of the world, but the family finally
settled in England. At thirteen, Margot
entered the Sadler's Wells School. Her
first appearance on stage was as one of
the thirty-two snowflakes in *The Nutcracker*. She passed quite unnoticed.

Alicia Markova was her idol and
ideal, and Margot studied every move
the great *prima* made, never thinking
she could come even close to her in
performance. When Markova left Sadler's Wells, however, Fonteyn began to
rise rapidly. At seventeen she danced
Giselle, and her sensitive interpretation
of the role left no doubt that here was
a new *prima ballerina*.

It might be said that Michael Somes is
Michael Somes the King of the
Royal Ballet. His
title is *premier danseur noble,* and he
has been Margot Fonteyn's partner for
many years. He was the first boy to win
a scholarship to Sadler's Wells. His
manly appearance, noble air and skill
have enhanced every role he has under-
taken. His dancing career was inter-
rupted by four years of distinguished

service in the British army — with no
impairment to his art.

A truly American Queen of Ballet is
Maria Tallchief Maria Tallchief.
She was born on an
Osage reservation in Oklahoma. Her
father is an Indian, her mother of
Scottish descent. Enormously talented,
she first studied piano. At twelve she
began serious study of ballet with the
sister of Nijinsky, and before long, the
dance became her first love. Later,
George Balanchine had much to do with
perfecting her technique.

Maria Tallchief has tremendous
power as a dancer, but it is always under
perfect control. Her leaps in the air
are phenomenal, her *entrechats* fabu-
lous. She can beat her legs together
eight times in a dazzling twinkle of
perfect form. Only Nijinsky could
better that, and his record was ten. Her
style is classic elegance tipped with fire;
her performances are unforgettable.

Although he is considered an American
André Eglevsky dancer, André
Eglevsky was born
in Moscow. He studied in Paris with
Volinine, one of Pavlova's partners,
and in London with Nicholas Legat,
also of Diaghilev's famous company.
He made his debut at the age of fifteen
with the rank of *premier danseur*.

Eglevsky is tall and rather heavily
built, but he has a catlike grace and an
exceptional jumping ability. In his soar-
ing leaps, he, too, can create the illusion of being suspended in mid-air.

When, at the age of eight, little Alicia

Alicia Alonso

was sent to a ballet school in Havana, it was to acquire poise and grace. There was no thought of making a ballerina of her. Such a career was considered unthinkable for the daughter of a prominent Cuban family. But Alicia's talent could not be denied and eventually she continued her studies at the School of American Ballet in New York. She became a *prima ballerina* of Ballet Theater, but she and her husband also founded the Ballet Alicia Alonso. This later became known as Ballet de Cuba, which was government-supported.

Her artistic range is amazing. She can be the glittering Black Swan or the gentle heroine of *Romeo and Juliet,* for she is an accomplished actress as well as a dancer.

Some years ago she was threatened with blindness. A series of operations followed, and for a year she lay in bed, her eyes bandaged, forbidden even to cry for fear of the effect of such emotion on the delicate nerves and tissues that needed healing.

Yet she did not waste time in self-pity. Instead, Alicia visualized in her active mind every role she had danced, and so clearly that she was able to pick out what she regarded as flaws in her performances. The healing ordeal over, there was the matter of restoring her flabby muscles. Alicia's courage never flagged. When she returned to the stage it was to further triumphs as a more mature, more glorious *prima,* who had now also earned the title of *Dama,* the highest honor bestowed by Cuba on a civilian.

ALICIA ALONSO and IGOR YOUSKEVITCH

MARIA TALLCHIEF

MARGOT FONTEYN
and
MICHAEL SOMES

The Prince dances with Cinderella while her stepsisters observe them.

A virtuoso is one who has special
Igor Youskevitch knowledge or skill in any field. In ballet, Igor Youskevitch is considered not only a virtuoso but also a genius. He was trained as an athlete in Yugoslavia, but turned to ballet while at the university in Belgrade. Although usually it takes years to perfect ballet technique, this young man was able to perform after only a year of formal study. He dances with virile elegance and is the favorite partner of Alicia Alonso. During the war he served with the United States Navy.

Illinois-born John Kriza studied in Chi-
John Kriza cago and made his debut in the Chicago Opera Ballet. His first outstanding success was as one of the sailors in *Fancy Free*. He is especially well suited to ballets with American themes and has danced in Agnes De Mille's *Rodeo* and Eugene Loring's *Billy the Kid*.

John Kriza (right) dances in the ballet *Billy the Kid*.

What It Takes to Be a Ballet Dancer

Having read about the dancers of yesterday and today, you know that it is not easy to become a great performer. Since many years of specialized physical training are involved, one of the requirements is good physical condition. However, there are exceptions to all rules, and some of our finest dancers began studying *because* of handicaps.

Alicia Markova, one of the greatest ballerinas in the world, was ordered to

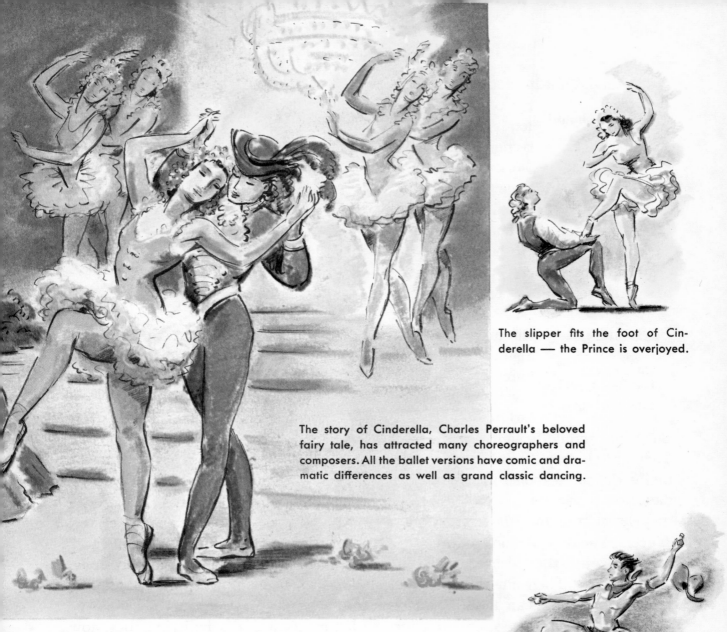

The slipper fits the foot of Cinderella — the Prince is overjoyed.

The story of Cinderella, Charles Perrault's beloved fairy tale, has attracted many choreographers and composers. All the ballet versions have comic and dramatic differences as well as grand classic dancing.

Eugene Loring's *Billy the Kid* is a favorite modern American ballet.

take ballet lessons by her family doctor. She was frail and had knock-knees. But ballet discipline and carefully supervised exercises cured her ailments — and her talent was uncovered for all the world to see.

Nana Gollner's limbs had been weakened by polio and ballet was suggested as a means of strengthening them. Her progress was so rapid that by the age of sixteen she attained the rank of *prima ballerina*.

Marie Taglioni, with long arms and a hunch in her back, was built all wrong for a ballerina. Although her father was

so ambitious for her, it may be that he also knew what ballet training could do for a frail, unbeautiful body.

But these are the *exceptions*. Ordinarily, people don't start ballet studies with such handicaps. Certainly one should have a good, strong heart, a sense of rhythm, a feeling for music and an overpowering desire to dance.

Ballet should not be studied before the age of eight. Nine or ten is not too late to begin either. Toe work should never be attempted before the age of ten, and then *only after* three years of study with a competent teacher. That much time is needed to strengthen the foot, leg and back muscles properly; otherwise, serious permanent injuries can result.

How old should one be to take ballet lessons?

Boys and girls often take classes together, but there are some things which are taught to them separately. Ballerinas should be light and graceful. They must be supple and they do, eventually, dance on their toes. Boys never dance on their toes. Many of the steps they learn resemble those of the girl dancers, but they are done in a manly way. Boys are trained as partners for the ballerinas. Their muscles are developed so that they can lift a ballerina shoulder-high without apparent effort — not an easy thing to do, for she may weigh one hundred pounds or more. Being stronger than girls, they can leap higher and wider.

How does ballet training for boys and girls differ?

There is nothing "sissy" about ballet dancing for a boy. If you have the chance to observe boys taking class, you will see how much endurance is required of them. Incidentally, many of our foremost dancers have had excellent war records and were decorated and accorded other honors for their outstanding courage.

Although at one time the *danseur's* role had shrunk so that he was called "the ballerina's third leg," times have changed. All he did then was to support her and wear an admiring expression on his face. There is much more to being a partner today. Of course, the *danseur* must always be the cavalier and show a proper gallantry toward the ballerina, but now there is far greater depth in his roles. He must not only be an excellent dancer, but also a dramatic actor—as Albrecht in *Giselle* or Prince Siegfried in *Swan Lake,* for example.

What is the role of the *danseur*?

Some of the men, including Eglevsky and Youskevitch, have such outstanding talent that parts are especially written for them. A good *danseur* is a welcome addition to any company.

Ballet Dress

The simplest costumes are best for class.

What is the costume for the class? Girls wear jersey leotards over their tights (without feet, because they last longer that way), ankle socks and practice shoes. Some schools favor a short tunic for girls. Boys wear tights also and a jersey shirt. Their practice shoes are sometimes held over the instep by an elastic band.

In order to correct faults, a teacher must easily see the lines and movements of the body. Frills, bows, pleats and ruffles would conceal such faults. And tights also serve to keep the leg muscles warm. More injuries result from cold muscles than from any other cause. (That is one reason why baseball players wear full uniforms instead of shorts and tee-shirts.)

Another reason why boys wear tights instead of regular trousers is to give them unhindered movement.

The dancer's feet are her most precious **How are ballet slippers made?** equipment, and so dance shoes must always fit perfectly. They must never be bought to "grow into." The black ballet slippers are made of soft leather, with the toes pleated on the bottom, and with flexible, nonskid soles.

The satin toe shoes should not be heavy and hard and stiff. The well-prepared student can easily work in the soft, Italian-type shoes, which are hand-sewn and only lightly boxed. The dancer must at all times be able to "feel" the floor. Toe shoes are darned at the tips not only to make them grip the floor better, but also to make them last longer. Toe shoes are expensive, and professional dancers sometimes wear out several pairs during a single performance.

The stage costumes of today vary **What kind of stage costumes are used?** greatly in design. Besides the traditional, long romantic *tutu* and the short classic *tutu*, there are hundreds of variations, limited only by the subject of the ballet and the designers' imagination.

Costumes for the *danseurs* are varied, too, from the accepted classic tights and velvet jerkin to anything the part may call for — a Roman toga, a full-

COPPÉLIA

A light-hearted story and an excellent example of ballet pantomime is *Coppélia*. It involves a romance between Franz and a life-like doll which almost ends his courtship of Swanilda, a very real young lady. All the difficulties get solved, however, and the ballet closes with a *divertissement* or a sequence of steps.

dress suit, a business suit, or a bathing suit as in the ballet *Jones Beach*.

National costumes for character dancing are adapted for ballet use also. Their purpose is only to give an authentic flavor, and they are not intended to be replicas of native dress.

Ballet Talk

Since ballet, as we know it, came to us from France, most of the language of the ballet is also French. But some of the terms are derived from the Italian, because the early forms of ballet were brought to France from Italy. Inevitably, the country where ballet happens to be studied, adds its own vocabulary. In the main, however, students everywhere in the world learn the same terms.

ON STAGE!

The one-act modern ballet *On Stage!* will give you a behind-the-scenes glimpse of a rehearsal and an audition. There is a very grand ballerina in it and several young hopefuls, including the one who is not hired at first, but who finally wins a place in the company, too.

COQ D'OR, OR THE GOLDEN COCKEREL

The ballet *Coq D'or,* or *The Golden Cockerel,* is based on a poem by the Russian writer Aleksander Pushkin. Old King Dodon is given a marvelous golden cockerel which always warns him of coming danger. Along with the superb dancing, there are beautiful costumes and scenery; the whole is a spectacle.

Therefore, German, Italian, Danish, Swedish, Russian and English dancers, as well as performers from other nations, can step into class in any other country and proceed with the lesson in progress without too much misunderstanding. The teacher will call for the steps in ballet's universal language.

Labanotation—Dance in Writing

How can dance movements be written down?

Labanotation is a method for writing down dance movements, originated by Rudolf Laban. It can be compared to writing music, because a staff and symbols are used to "spell out" the movements which are to be performed. Those who understand this method can read and study dance scores no matter what language they speak.

Any and all movements can be recorded — even the fluttering of the fingers. It is hoped in the near future to have a whole generation of ballet score readers. To that end, young children in England, Holland, Brazil, Chile, Australia, Iceland and the United States are being taught to reconstruct dances from Labanotation. Here is a sample of how it works:

1. *Body:* A vertical staff is used to indicate the body. It represents you, the dancer. The center line is *your* center line, so that the right leg, arm, shoulder, etc., are written on the right side of the staff. The left parts of your body are shown on the left side of the staff.

There is a column for each part of the body, and the direction symbol is placed in the proper column to show which part is to move.

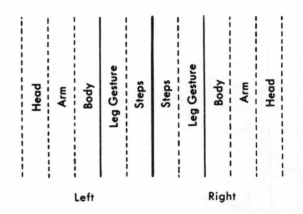

2. *Directions:* In the middle, at your center is "place" (no direction). This is shown by a rectangle: ☐

By changing this shape, the symbol is made to point to the directions around you — forward, backward, right, left and the four diagonal directions that are in between.

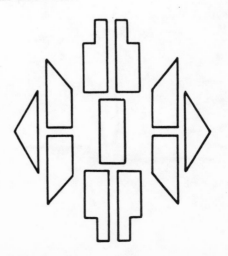

3. *Levels:* The level, meaning how high or how low, is shown by shading the symbol. Black is low (down toward the earth); a dot means horizontal or "middle" level; and stripes mean high, upward (toward the sky).

4. *Timing:* How long a movement lasts is shown by the length of the movement symbol. A slow movement will be written with a long symbol, a fast movement with a short symbol. The center line of the staff also represents time going by as you read it going up the page, and so a slow movement will take a lot of space on the time line.

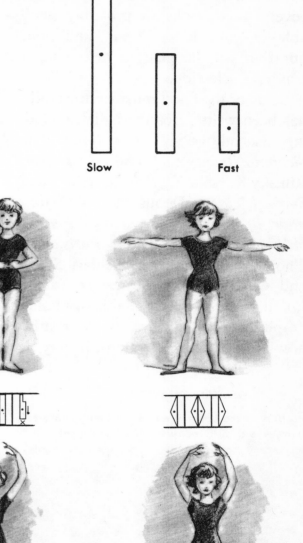

Slow   Fast

The five basic ballet positions, and all other dance movements, can be recorded in written form by *Labanotation*.

How You Can Enjoy Ballet

To help you become even more familiar with this dance form, reading other books about ballet, famous ballet dancers or stories about girls and boys in ballet can be a worthwhile experience. Several good books are probably available at your local library and your librarian will be glad to help you in making a selection.

Some of the finest music in the world has been written for the ballet, including Tschaikovsky's *Swan Lake, The Sleeping Beauty* and *The Nutcracker;* Rimsky-Korsakov's *Scheherazade* and *Snow Maiden;* Debussy's *The Afternoon of a Faun;* Stravinsky's *Petrouchka;* Offenbach's *Gaité Parisienne;* Chopin's *Les Sylphides;* Delibes' *Sylvia* and *Coppélia;* and Strauss' *Pizzicato Polka.* This music is available on phonograph records, and since many libraries now have record collections, it may be possible for you to borrow a recording as you would a book. Some libraries also have facilities for listening to records in a music room.

However, nothing can take the place of a real live ballet performance. Good ballet schools in your vicinity may give public recitals. Or there may be a college near you with a dance department that schedules regular concert performances. Best of all, if a ballet company comes to your town, or nearby, see the production if you can.

But before you go, find out which ballet will be performed. Then look up the story of that particular ballet in a book. Knowing the plot in advance will help you to understand the actions of the dancers. Thus prepared, you will really be able to enter the wonderful world of ballet — a world of magnificent music, drama, art and magical dancing that will hold you spellbound.

"Are those people really real?" you, too, may feel like asking. And who knows — some day a boy or girl may be asking his mother or father the same question about *you!*

WESTERN SYMPHONY

There is no story in the ballet *Western Symphony.* Rather, it is a Western scene depicting cowboy life. Brilliant color, brilliant costumes and catchy music give it a special quality.